Rio de Janeiro Travel Guide

Top 10 Things to See and Do

Anna Fichter

Table of Content

Introduction to Rio de Janeiro

Welcome to Rio de Janeiro, one of the world's most active and engaging urban areas! This book is planned to help you in benefiting from your visit to Rio, whether you're a successive explorer or a first-time guest.

Rio de Janeiro, with its stunning sea shores, verdant slopes, samba music, and festival energy, is a city that enraptures the creative mind. There is no absence of things to see and do around here, from notable attractions like Christ the Deliverer and Sugarloaf Mountain to the energetic neighbourhoods of Copacabana and Ipanema.

We'll walk you through the best ten sights and exercises in Rio de Janeiro in this aide. We'll go through the city's beautiful attractions, social diamonds, and notable landmarks as well as give exhortation on the most proficient method to orchestrate your timetable and boost your time there.

Set yourself up to encounter Rio de Janeiro's enthusiastic energy and investigate what this city brings to the table.

Christ the Redeemer

Christ the Hero is both one of Rio de Janeiro's most glaring landmarks and an impressive accomplishment. The landmark, which stands 30 metres (98 feet) tall and overlooks the city from Corcovado Mountain, provides breathtaking views of Rio de Janeiro's urban landscape and the surrounding typical brightness. The details of visiting Christ the Deliverer, such as how to arrive, how much the trip will cost, and what to expect while there, will all be covered in this section.

Region

Christ the Deliverer is located in the Tijuca Recreational Area, near the summit of Corcovado Mountain. The mountain is situated in Rio de Janeiro's southern neighbourhood and is accessible from many locations. The most popular and often used way to travel to Christ the Rescuer is by taking the stuffed tooth train from the Cosme Velho station. The 20-minute train ride offers breathtaking views of the blending urban and rural surroundings. Visitors may also go to the landmark via taxi or other means of transportation, albeit these options may be less convenient and require more time.

Ticket prices

There are two unique methods to purchase tickets for Christ the Friend in Need: online or at the ticket desk at the train line station. You might buy tickets online at the Power website. The price of the tickets is influenced by the time of year and if you choose a scheduled visit. Costs for one person fluctuate between R$82 (about $15) and R$123 (around $23).

The railway station's ticket office is open from 8 am to 6 pm and you may purchase your tickets up to two hours before the final train departs if you'd want to do so. Although there may be long waits and queues to purchase tickets during peak hours and on weekends, prices in the movie industry are the same as those found online.

Visit from Christ the Deliverer

You will be greeted with the majestic image of Christ the Hero as you arrive at Corcovado Mountain's highest point. Visitors may walk around the base of the statue and enjoy the spectacular views of Rio de Janeiro. The fact that the milestone may be involved, especially during workdays and events during peak season, is fundamentally noteworthy.

If you're interested in more deeply focusing on the foundation and significance of Christ the Deliverer, coordinated trips are provided at an additional cost. Expert middlemen who are knowledgeable about Brazil's and Rio de Janeiro's arrangements for meetings as well as the relevance of the model organise the visits.

It's also important to keep in mind that the surroundings at Corcovado Mountain's peak are fanciful and that the landmark sometimes seems to be obscured by darkness or fog. But even on foggy days, the mountain's highest peak offers breathtaking views that make the journey worthwhile.

The direction of Christ the Angel of Protection's appearance

You will benefit more from your trip to Christ the Deliverer if you go with the direction:

Decide on a plan of action and advance your tickets beyond the time limit to avoid extended pauses and arrangements.

Consider leaving quickly during the morning or evening hours if you want to avoid the crowds.

Bring a variety of sturdy walking shoes, and be prepared to climb stairs and go uphill.

Check the weather patterns at Corcovado Mountain's summit, and be prepared for changing weather conditions.

Bring a camera so you can capture the magnificent picture and historic moment.

Christ the Guardian angel should be seen by everyone who travels to Rio de Janeiro. The landmark serves as both a representation of the city and a sign of Brazil's diverse socioeconomic history. Whether visitors are captivated by the architecture, symbolism, or breathtaking views, Christ the Hero makes sure to have an impact on everyone who comes.

Sugarloaf Mountain

The Sugarloaf Mountain, otherwise called Po do Açcar in Portuguese, is one of Rio de Janeiro's most well-known vistas. Anybody who needs to encounter the city's incredible significance and amazing scenes ought to visit. The data you want to visit Sugarloaf Mountain, including its area, affirmation expenses, and what to expect while there, will be shrouded in this segment.

Region

You can find Sugarloaf Mountain in the Urca region, which is in Rio de Janeiro's southern area. Astonishing perspectives on the city and its environmental elements are made conceivable by the mountain's particular design and area at the mouth of the Guanabara River.

To get to Sugarloaf Mountain, guests might take a trolley from the base station, which is arranged at the mountain's base. The two-segment cable car ride incorporates a stop at the little pinnacle known as Morro da Urca, which is generally up Sugarloaf. Voyagers might land at Morro da Urca to take in the view and investigate the area before proceeding with their excursion to Sugarloaf Mountain's pinnacle.

Ticket costs

There is an assortment of ticket choices accessible for individuals who should visit Sugarloaf Mountain. You might purchase tickets on the web or at the base station's ticket counter. Contingent upon the season, costs per individual might change from R$90 (about $17) to R$110 (around $21).

There are additionally directed visits accessible, which could give more insider data on the mountain's significance and past. The expense of a coordinated visit differs relying on how the visit is run and how long the trip endures.

Visiting Sugarloaf Mountain out travelling

When you arrive at the highest point of Sugarloaf Mountain, you will be invited with dazzling widely inclusive perspectives across Rio de Janeiro and its encompasses. Well-known metropolitan milestones including Christ the Deliverer, Copacabana Oceanside, and Guanabara Straight might be seen in this area. There are numerous perception decks and review towers that give fluctuated vantage points of the city and its environmental elements at the culmination of the mountain.

Guests may likewise investigate the environmental elements of Sugarloaf Zenith, for example, the little Morro da Urca top, which offers a comparably gorgeous vista. There are a few strolling ways and trails in and around Morro da Urca, giving an open door to investigate the region and take in the landscape.

Counsel On the most proficient method to Get to Sugarloaf Mountain

The accompanying counsel will assist you with taking advantage of your excursion to Sugarloaf Mountain:

Make arrangements and buy your tickets ahead of time to stay away from extensive arrangements and postponements.

Think about leaving right promptly in the first part of the day or at night to stay away from the gatherings.

Put on comfortable shoes so you can go uphill and arrange steps.

By truly taking a gander at the weather conditions figure, you might be prepared for moving weather conditions at the highest point of the mountain.

Bring a camera so you might catch the region's stunning landscape and untainted magnificence.

Guests to Rio de Janeiro need to try visiting Sugarloaf Mountain. Because of its stunning scenes, remarkable area, and steady significance, it is likely the most well-known site in the city. In any case matter how energetic you are about the district's variety of exercises, stunning perspectives, or regular quality, Sugarloaf Mountain is sure to make an effect on every individual who comes. Visiting Sugarloaf Mountain, a staple of any excursion to Rio de Janeiro, gives an assortment of visit choices, moderate ticket evaluation, and direct travel choices. So make certain to remember this notable area for your timetable and experience Sugarloaf Mountain's gloriousness for yourself.

Copacabana Beach

Perhaps of the most extraordinary shoreline on the planet, the Copacabana Coastline is a serious need locale for pilgrims visiting Rio de Janeiro. It is a notable goal for the two guests and inhabitants to think about the best approach to its great shore, white sand, and clear water. All that you require to be familiar with visiting the Copacabana Ocean side, including its area, assertion expenses, and what the future holds while there, will be battled in this part.

Locale

Between the Copacabana and Leme locales, in the southern area of Rio de Janeiro, is where you'll track down the Copacabana Ocean side. Tall design plans, restaurants and stores flank the 4.5 km of coastline that crosses down the shore.

Guests could take a taxi, transport, or underground to the nearest station, Cardeal Arcoverde, and consequently head out beginning there to the Copacabana Coastline. The ocean side is only a short leave by then.

Ticket costs

Since the Copacabana Ocean side is a public coastline, there are no extra charges. Notwithstanding, several transporters along the ocean side will offer seats and umbrellas to visitors at a cost. Rental charges for seats and umbrellas change thinking about the transporter and the season yet by and large expenses are put in the extent of $2 and $4 per thing or R$10 to R$20 per thing.

Copacabana Ocean side journey

Copacabana Ocean Side invites you with dumbfounding perspectives on the coastline and blazing ocean. There are many parts of the ocean side, each with its point of view and demeanour.

Avenida Atlantica and the encompassing region of the shoreline are where travellers could find the most vendors offering food, prizes, and miscellaneous items. Different bistros and bistros can be found along this stretch of the ocean side, where visitors could eat and drink while esteeming the stunning point of view.

There are two or three opportunities for water sports fans, including surfing, paddleboarding, and kayaking. Guests could take a directed visit to push extra about the district or lease gear from dealers along the ocean side.

Course for Pilgrims to Copacabana Shoreline

The Going with direction will assist you with taking advantage of your excursion to the Copacabana Coastline:

Dress delicately and put on ocean side-fitting footwear.

Put on sunscreen and a cap to protect yourself from the sun.

Take the necessary steps not to pass on your assets unattended on the ocean front to keep them secure.

Bring a great deal of water, and drink stores of it.

Have some experience with your normal parts and see the provincial culture and customs.

Anybody visiting Rio de Janeiro ought to endeavour to visit the Copacabana Ocean side. It is viewed as one of the most choice sea shores on earth because of its amazing shore, fine white sand, and clear water. Copacabana Ocean Side has polished for all interests, including shopping, sunbathing, and water sports.

Visits to the Copacabana Ocean side are an irrefutable need on each excursion to Rio de Janeiro in light of the essential access through open travel, the expense-free entry, and the surge of shops and cafés there. So make a point to recall this prominent ocean side for your timetable and find Copacabana's magnificence for yourself!

Ipanema Beach

Ipanema Seaside, one of Rio de Janeiro's most intense coastlines, is frequently of significant enticement for globe-trotters. With its white sand, clear water, and amazing perspectives on the city, it isn't to be expected that this oceanside has drawn in travellers from everywhere in the world. This segment will cover all you need to be familiar with visiting the Ipanema Oceanside, including its area, confirmation expenses, and what's on the horizon while you're there.

Region

Ipanema Seaside is situated in Rio de Janeiro's southern district, only south of the Copacabana Seaside. The 2.6 km long seaside, which is coordinated along the shore, is populated by individuals of all financial classes in Ipanema and Leblon.

To get to the Ipanema Sea side, guests could utilize a taxi, public travel or the metro to the nearest station, Ipanema/General Osorio. The separation starting there to the sea is somewhat short.

Ticket costs

Ipanema Sea side is allowed to visit and accessible to the whole open. By the by, various organizations on the beachfront charge clients for seats and umbrellas. Albeit the expense to lease seats and umbrellas changes relying upon the merchant and the season, it commonly goes somewhere in the range of $2 and $4 per thing or R$10 and R$20 per thing.

Visiting the oceanside of Ipanema

Ipanema water side invites you with amazing perspectives on the shore and shimmering water. Each part of the oceanside has its extraordinary viewpoint and disposition.

The most notable part of the oceanside, Posto 9, is prominent for its cheery environment and straightforward culture. This segment of the oceanside is popular with the two inhabitants and guests, and it's an extraordinary spot to human watch and absorbs the sun.

Water sports devotees have a decision a few exercises, including surfing, paddleboarding, and kayaking. Guests could join a directed visit to advance additional about the area or lease hardware from organizations along the coast.

Moreover, Ipanema Seaside is home to various restaurants and bistros where visitors might unwind with dinner or a beverage while respecting the stunning perspective. Everybody can find something they like, whether they pick nearby top choices or top suggestions generally speaking.

Ipanema Sea side visitor bearing

You might take full advantage of your excursion to the Ipanema Ocean side by pursuing the course and way:

Put on savvy clothing and real ocean-side shoes.

Wear a cap and sunscreen to safeguard yourself from the sun.

Avoid the potential risk to forestall leaving your resources close to the water unattended to protect them.

Bring a lot of water and chug it down.

Find out about your ordinary impacts and notice the close by societies and propensities.

Everybody visiting Rio de Janeiro ought to set aside some margin to visit the Ipanema Seaside. Due to its tremendous coastline, fine white sand, and clear water, it is viewed as quite possibly of the most gorgeous beach in the world. There are exercises for all interests on the Ipanema Sea side, like shopping, tanning, and water sports. Each outing to Rio de Janeiro incorporates a stop to the Ipanema Ocean side since it gives fast access by improvement, a free part, and an enormous assortment of shops and cafés. So make it a highlight remember Ipanema for your arrangements and find its significance for yourself!

Tijuca National Park

For everybody inspired by the outside and natural life, Tijuca Public Park is one of Rio de Janeiro's most staggering and popular attractions. This segment will cover all the data you want to visit Tijuca Public Park, including its area, confirmation expenses, and what to expect while there.

Area

With an all-out size of around 39 square kilometres, Tijuca Public Park is arranged in the focal point of Rio de Janeiro. The recreation area is near all regions of the city and is encircled by the networks of Tijuca, Alto da Boa Vista, thus Conrado.

Guests might take a taxi or public travel to one of the recreation area's entryways to get to Tijuca Public Park. The Guest Community at Alto da Boa Vista, which is open regularly from 8 am to 5 pm, has the most active section.

Ticket costs

Contingent upon your arrangements and the districts you wish to investigate, there are an assortment of ticket decisions for visiting Tijuca Public Park. The overall passage ticket, which empowers guests to investigate the recreation area's climbing trails, cascades, and vistas, is the most frequently utilized ticket type. A standard confirmation ticket will slow down your R$34 (around $6) per individual.

Guests might purchase tickets for specific exercises like jeep trips, rock climbing, and shelter visits notwithstanding the essential entry ticket. Contingent upon the merchant and the season, these exercises ordinarily cost somewhere in the range of R$100 and R$300 (about $20 and $60) per individual.

Tijuca Public Park visit

You'll be invited by lavish woods, eminent cascades, and astonishing city vistas when you enter Tijuca Public Park. Different climbing courses in the recreation area go from short walks around exhausting climbs and take you to some of Rio de Janeiro's most stunning areas.

The Pico da Tijuca climb, which rises to Tijuca Pinnacle and gives all-encompassing perspectives on the city and the encompassing mountains, is perhaps the most popular path in the recreation area. It requires around 2-3 hours to cross the 3.8-kilometre-long trip.

The Cascatinha Cascade, another popular objective in Tijuca Public Park, is promptly available to the guest community. A little walk will carry guests to the cascade, where they might chill off in the normal pool beneath.

Tijuca Public Park gives different chances to daredevils, including jeep rides, rock climbing, and shelter visits. These pursuits are fabulous ways of partaking in the excitement of experience while finding the recreation area's regular magnificence.

Guest Guidance for the Tijuca Public Park

The accompanying counsel will assist you with benefiting from your excursion to Tijuca Public Park:

Put on loosened-up garments and climbing suitable, durable shoes.

Wear sunscreen and bug splash to safeguard yourself from the sun and bugs.

Bring a lot of food and drink.

Regard the climate by abstaining from upsetting creatures or littering.

See all security precautionary measures while taking part in brave exercises, and pick a reliable seller.

Any individual who partakes in the outside and untamed life ought to visit Tijuca Public Park, a characteristic heaven situated in the focal point of Rio de Janeiro. The recreation area gives something to everybody, whether you're keen on climbing, experiencing sports, or simply absorbing Rio de Janeiro's normal magnificence with its rich woods, exquisite cascades, and marvellous vistas. A feature of every excursion to Rio de Janeiro is visiting Tijuca Public Park, which offers modest entry costs and functional travel choices. Thusly, make certain to remember this well-known area for your timetable and encounters.

Lapa Neighborhood

Guests might experience the city's clamouring nightlife and history by visiting the Lapa area in Rio de Janeiro. Any guest to Rio should see Lapa, with its conspicuous curves and samba clubs. Here are the best ten activities in Lapa, alongside subtleties on where they are and the amount they cost:

Arcos da Lapa - The Arcos da Lapa is a notable landmark in Rio de Janeiro. The dynamite water system, which crosses the Lapa area, was built in the eighteenth hundred years. For a wide-point viewpoint of the city, guests might go to the highest point of the curves. Area: Lapa, Rio de Janeiro, Rua Riachuelo. No charge.

Escadaria Selarón - Associating the Lapa and St Nick Teresa areas is the beautiful Escadaria Selarón flight of stairs. More than

2,000 distinct tiles, every one exceptional, cover the steps. The venture was started in 1990 by the craftsman Jorge Selarón, and it has since become one of Rio's most popular vacation locations. Area: Lapa, Rio de Janeiro, Rua Joaquim Silva. No charge.

Fundiço Progresso - The Fundiço Progresso is a social centre where plays, shows and craftsmanship displays are held. Anyone with any interest at all in Rio's music culture ought to visit the scene, which is set in a staggering workmanship deco structure. Area: Lapa, Rio de Janeiro, Rua dos Arcos, 24. Value: Contingent upon the occasion, it changes.

The Circo Voador is one of Rio de Janeiro's most prestigious music scenes. The absolute most prominent specialists from Brazil have performed in the open-air field, including Caetano Veloso and Gilberto Gil. At the Circo Voador, guests might feel the energy of Rio's unrecorded music scene. Area: Lapa, Rio de Janeiro, Rua dos Arcos, s/n. Value: Contingent upon the occasion, it differs.

A notable club in the Lapa area is called Lapa 40 Graus. The club highlights many floors with various melodic styles, like techno, funk, and samba. At Lapa 40 Graus, guests might move the night away. Area: Lapa, Rio de Janeiro, Rua Riachuelo, 97. Value: Contingent upon the evening, it changes.

Teresa Cristina and Monarco, two of Rio de Janeiro's most notable samba craftsmen, have acted in the samba club Carioca da Gema. The club is a fantastic spot to find Rio's samba culture and offers a comfortable climate. Area: Lapa, Rio de Janeiro, Av. Mem de Sá, 79. Value: Contingent upon the evening, it changes.

Rio Scenarium - Rio Scenarium is a sizable club situated in a pioneer home that has been revamped. Samba, jazz, and forró are among the melodic kinds played in the scene's few stories. The club has a few workmanship shows, making it a fabulous spot to see Rio's flourishing craftsmanship scene. Area: Lapa, Rio de Janeiro, 20 Rua do Lavradio. Value: Contingent upon the evening, it shifts.

Lapa Irish Bar - The Lapa Irish Bar is a comfortable bar that gives a difference in pace from the local's samba and funk clubs. Guinness and bar admission might be appreciated by visitors as they take in unrecorded music. Also, the bar conducts different exercises including test evenings. Area: Lapa, Rio de Janeiro, Rua Evaristo da Veiga, 147. Value: Contingent upon the evening, it fluctuates.

Feira do Lavradio - The primary Saturday of every month is the point at which the Feira do Lavradio road market is held. Various collectables, handiworks, and food merchants might be found at the market. At the market, visitors may likewise take in live diversion and road performers. Area: Lapa, Rio de Janeiro, Rua do Lavradio. Value: Allowed to investigate, nonetheless, buys have a scope of expenses.

Rio Scenarium Secondhand Store Shop - For people who like collectables, Rio Scenarium Secondhand Store Shop is a tremendous objective. An assortment of one-of-a-kind furnishings, craftsmanship, and enlivening things are accessible at the store. The store likewise sells old-fashioned attire and extras for guests. Area: Lapa, Rio de Janeiro, 20 Rua do Lavradio. Value: Contingent upon the thing, it shifts.

Lapa has a few diners and bistros that give both unfamiliar and conventional Brazilian food notwithstanding these main ten attractions. Guests might test po de queijo, a Brazilian cheddar bread, or feijoada, a commonplace Brazilian stew made with dark beans and pork. Also, some road merchants in Lapa sell average Brazilian desserts like coxinha and pastels.

Lapa is likewise home to a scope of housing choices, including spending plan inns and five-star resorts. The region offers economical other options, going with it a phenomenal decision for those on a limited financial plan.

Lapa is advantageously near the metro and transport lines concerning transportation. The Cinelândia metro station, which connects to various areas of Rio de Janeiro, offers support to the area. Transports may likewise be utilized by guests to go to Lapa from different regions of the city.

Anybody visiting Rio de Janeiro ought to make a point to stop at Lapa. The region gives a particular combination of history, culture, and nightlife that is unrivalled across the city. Lapa has something for everybody, from its conspicuous curves to its samba clubs.

Santa Teresa Neighborhood

One of Rio de Janeiro's cutest and most artistic neighbourhoods is Santa Teresa. Santa Teresa, which is perched on a hilltop with views of the city, presents tourists with a distinctive fusion of art, culture, and history. We'll look at the top ten things to do and see in Santa Teresa in this travel guide.

Parque das Runas is a cultural hub housed in a historic villa that formerly belonged to renowned Brazilian artist Laurinda Santos Lobo. Visitors may explore the centre's art exhibits and cultural activities while taking in the breathtaking city views from the mansion's roof. Location: Santa Teresa, Rio de Janeiro, Rua Murtinho Nobre, 169. No charge.

The Selarón Steps are a well-known tourist destination in Rio de Janeiro. Jorge Selarón, a Chilean artist, built the stairs, which are coated in bright tiles. Visitors may ascend the stairs and capture images of the vibrant artwork. Location: Santa Teresa, Rio de Janeiro, Rua Joaquim Silva. No charge.

Chácara do Céu Museum - The Raymundo Ottoni de Castro Maya, a Brazilian collector, formerly owned the stunning estate where the Chácara does Céu Museum is now located. The gallery houses a collection of European and Brazilian artwork, including pieces by Matisse, Portinari, and Di Cavalcanti. The lovely grounds around the home are also available for visitors to explore. Location: Santa Teresa, Rio de Janeiro, Rua Murtinho Nobre, 93. Adults pay R$ 8; elderly and students pay R$ 4, respectively.

Santa Teresa Tram: The Santa Teresa Tram travels through the neighbourhood and is a historic tram. The tram, which was first constructed in 1896, gives tourists a beautiful tour of Santa Teresa. Views of the neighbourhood's lovely streets and homes are available to visitors. Location: Santa Teresa, Rio de Janeiro, Rua Lélio Gama. Adults pay R$ 20; kids and elderly citizens pay R$ 10, respectively.

Museu da Imagem e do Som - The history of Brazilian film and music is the focus of the Museu da Imagem e do Som. Old records, pictures, and movie posters are on display in the museum. The museum hosts live musical concerts for visitors to enjoy. Location: Santa Teresa, Rio de Janeiro, Rua Visconde de Maranguape, 19. Adults pay R$ 6; students and elderly citizens pay R$ 3.

Escadaria Joo do Rio - A stairway decorated in vibrant tiles and graffiti is known as Escadaria Joo do Rio. The staircase bears Joo do Rio's name, a well-known author and journalist from Brazil. Visitors are welcome to ascend the stairs and capture images of the vibrant artwork. Location: Santa Teresa, Rio de Janeiro, Rua Joaquim Silva. No charge.

Feira de Antiguidades da Praça XV - Every Saturday, the Feira de Antiguidades da Praça XV is a market. A variety of antiques, handicrafts, and food vendors may be found at the market. At the market, guests may also take in live entertainment and street entertainers. Rio de Janeiro's Praça XV, close to Santa Teresa. Price: Free to explore, however, purchases have a range of costs.

Largo dos Guimares - In the centre of Santa Teresa, this picturesque plaza is called Largo dos Guimares. Restaurants, cafés and bars line all four sides of the area. Visitors may take pleasure in the energetic environment and sample some local delicacies. Location: Santa Teresa, Rio de

Janeiro's Largo dos Guimares. Price: The cost of meals and beverages varies.

The park known as Parque das Flores is situated right in the middle of Santa Teresa. There are several exotic plants and flowers in the park, in addition to a lovely waterfall. Visitors may take a stroll in the park and admire the scenery. Location: Santa Teresa, Rio de Janeiro, Rua Almirante Alexandrino. No charge.

The Santa Teresa Street Art Trip is a guided trip that takes people through Santa Teresa's streets to discover the area's thriving street art culture. In addition to admiring the vibrant murals and graffiti, visitors may discover more about the artists and their work. Location: The place to meet depends on the trip operator. Price: Depending on the trip operator, prices change.

A variety of cultural and artistic activities are available to tourists in the distinctive and endearing neighbourhood of Santa Teresa. Santa Teresa has something for everyone, whether they choose to walk the streets and take in the street art or explore the museums and cultural centres.

Rio Carnival

One of the most well-known events in the world, the Rio Carnival brings millions of tourists to Rio de Janeiro every year. The days before Lent are a time of song, dancing, and celebration during this vivacious and colourful festival of Brazilian culture. The top ten things to do and see during the Rio Carnival are listed below:

The Samba Parade, which is the highlight of the Rio Carnival, is a stunning show of dancing, music, and ornate costumes. The procession is held at the Sambadrome, a unique arena with a capacity of 90,000 spectators. Various samba schools contending for the title of Carnival Champion are included in each of the Samba Parade's divisions, which are separated into separate parades. Tickets for seeing the procession from the stands or

VIP boxes are available to the public. Location: Rio de Janeiro's Sambadrome on Avenida Marques de Sapucai. Cost: Prices for tickets begin at around R$500.

Blocos - Throughout the city, during Carnival, there are street celebrations known as 'Blocos'. These are casual get-togethers when people dance, sing, and rejoice. There are hundreds of Blocos available, each with a unique theme and musical genre. Blocos like Banda de Ipanema, Cordo da Bola Preta, and Monobloco are some of the most well-known. Location: Rio de Janeiro's many neighbourhoods. No charge.

Carnival Balls - The magnificent Carnival Balls are held in some of Rio's most stunning locations. These occasions include dancing, live music, and formal attire. The Magic Ball, the Gay Ball, and the Scala Ball are a few of the most well-known Carnival balls. Location: Rio de Janeiro's many venues. Cost: Prices for tickets begin at around R$500.

Rio de Janeiro is renowned for its thriving street art movement, and the city is covered in colourful murals and graffiti during Carnival. Some of the city's most well-known street art, such as the murals in the Santa Teresa neighbourhood and the graffiti in the Lapa district, may be seen on a walking tour. Location: Rio de Janeiro's many neighbourhoods. No charge.

The history and culture of the Rio Carnival are the focus of the Carnival Museum. The museum has displays on the development of Carnival costumes, the history of samba, and the significance of Carnival in Brazilian culture. Visitors may also see exhibits of vintage Carnival floats and attire. Location: 52-Centro Rua Marques de Sapucai, Rio de Janeiro. Cost: Prices for tickets begin at around R$20.

Food sellers selling customary Brazilian snacks and beverages line the streets of Rio de Janeiro during the Carnival. Delicious street foods like coxinhas (fried chicken croquettes), churros, and pastel de feira (deep-fried pastries stuffed with meat or cheese) are available for visitors to taste. Location: Rio de Janeiro's many neighbourhoods. Snacks and beverages start at around R$5.

Concerts during the Carnival - The Carnival is a musical occasion, and guests may attend performances by some of Brazil's best musicians. Several concerts are happening all across the city, including appearances by samba schools, well-known singers, and foreign performers. Location: Rio de Janeiro's many venues. Cost: Prices for tickets begin at around R$50.

Rio Carnival 5K - During the Carnival, there is a fun run called the Rio Carnival 5K. Running in bright costumes is encouraged, and the race begins and ends at the Sambadrome. After the race, there is a gathering with beverages and live music. The Rio Carnival 5K is a fantastic chance to get some exercise and see the Carnival from a fresh angle. Location: Rio de Janeiro's Sambadrome on Avenida Marques de Sapucai. Cost: The first registration price is around R$ 70.

Street Parties During Carnival - In addition to the Blocos, there are a lot of street parties happening all around the city. These gatherings, which are free and accessible to everyone, provide a more informal setting than the official events. At the street celebrations for Carnival, guests may take in music, dancing and street food. Location: Rio de Janeiro's many neighbourhoods. No charge.

Carnival Post-Party - Following the conclusion of the major Carnival festivities, the celebrations continue in the pubs and clubs of the city. Visitors are welcome to join the residents in celebrating the conclusion of the Carnival by dancing, drinking and listening to live music. The Lapa district and the bars in the Copacabana area are some of the top destinations for post-Carnival celebrations. Location: Rio de Janeiro's many neighbourhoods. Price: Varies according to the location.

A once-in-a-lifetime opportunity, the Rio Carnival should not be missed. From the formal Samba Parade to the more laid-back Blocos and street parties, visitors may take in a range of festivities. Visitors are likely to have an amazing experience at the Rio Carnival since there is so much to see and do.

Maracanã Stadium

Estádio do Maracan, frequently known as Maracan Arena, is quite possibly of the most conspicuous game fields on the planet. The arena, which is situated in Rio de Janeiro, Brazil, has played home to the absolute most eminent athletic events ever, including the opening and shutting services of the 2016 Summer Olympics and the 1950 FIFA World Cup last. Here are the best ten vacation destinations at Maracan Arena.

Guests to the arena might take a directed visit to find out about its set of experiences and view its insides very close. Admittance to the storage spaces, public interview room, celebrity segments, as well as an excursion through the passage onto the field, is completely remembered for the visit. Area: Maracan, Rio de Janeiro, Rua Teacher Eurico Rabelo. Tickets start at around R$60.

The Exhibition Hall of Football, housed inside Maracan Arena, gives a careful outline of Brazilian football history. The most celebrated competitors and groups in the country are featured, and guests might investigate intelligent presentations, see uncommon curios, and find out about them. Area: Maracan, Rio de Janeiro, Rua Teacher Eurico Rabelo. Cost: Costs for tickets start at around R$20.

Go to a Football Match-up - Flamengo and Fluminense, two of Brazil's most notable football crews, play their home games at Maracan Arena. To encounter the charging environment of a Brazilian football match-up, sightseers might go to a game. Area: Maracan, Rio de Janeiro, Rua Teacher Eurico Rabelo. Value: Ticket costs shift concurring on the game and the seat.

Move to the Top - Guests might climb to the arena's pinnacle for a stunning 360-degree scene of Rio de Janeiro. The sights merit the work regardless of whether the ascension is hard for the weak-willed. Area: Maracan, Rio de Janeiro, Rua Teacher Eurico Rabelo. Tickets start at around R$40.

Sports Shop - The arena's games shop offers a tremendous assortment of football-related items. The shop sells everything, including footballs, memorabilia, and group shirts. Area: Maracan, Rio de Janeiro, Rua Teacher Eurico Rabelo. Value: The expense of the merchandise changes.

Food Court - The arena's food court gives a scope of eating decisions, including inexpensive food, unfamiliar cooking, and customary Brazilian cooking styles. Guests might eat or nibble while absorbing the feel of the arena. Area: Maracan, Rio de Janeiro,

Rua Teacher Eurico Rabelo. Costs for food could change.

Jungle gym - The jungle gym at the arena offers an assortment of climbing designs, swings, and slides for youngsters to appreciate. While their kids play, guardians might unwind and take in the view. Area: Maracan, Rio de Janeiro, Rua Teacher Eurico Rabelo. No charge.

Shows - The Drifters, Madonna, and U2 were among the best melodic demonstrations to perform at Maracan Arena. If a show is arranged when a guest is there, they might look at the arena's timetable. Area: Maracan, Rio de Janeiro, Rua Teacher Eurico Rabelo. Value: Ticket costs shift concurring on the demonstration and the seat.

Bicycle Visit - A bicycle visit through Rio de Janeiro is accessible, and it incorporates a visit to Maracan Arena. The outing likewise incorporates a stop at the arena and a ride around the city's areas. Area: Rio de Janeiro's numerous areas.

Guests might hold a celebrity bundle that incorporates admittance to the arena's most selective segments, a customized visit, and top-of-the-line seats for a football match-up for a vital encounter. Area: Maracan, Rio de Janeiro, Rua Teacher Eurico Rabelo. Value: The expense of a celebrity bundle shifts concurring on its elements and level of selectiveness.

For anyone with any interest at all in Brazilian culture and history, as well as sports fans, Maracan Arena is a must-visit area. Everyone might find something to appreciate at Maracan Arena on account of its rich history and contemporary offices. Guests might circumvent the arena, watch a game, eat, or simply take in the fantastic perspectives. It is justifiable why Maracan

Arena is viewed as quite possibly the most conspicuous brandishing ground in the entire globe.

Museums and Cultural Centers

Rio de Janeiro is eminent for its amazing regular magnificence, invigorating nightlife, and broad history and culture. There are a few galleries and social organizations in the city, every one of which gives a particular window into Brazil's set of experiences and present. The main ten social foundations and galleries in Rio de Janeiro are recorded beneath:

The Exhibition Hall of Tomorrow is a state-of-the-art logical historical centre that looks at the improvement of the universe and the issues that our planet is presently encountering. It is arranged in the focal point of Rio de Janeiro. Current shows and intelligent showcases at the historical centre make it a must-visit area for science enthusiasts, everything being equal. Area:

Rio de Janeiro, Praça Mauá, 1 Centro. Cost: R$20 for general entry.

Rio de Janeiro Gallery of Workmanship (Blemish): The Exhibition Hall of Specialty of Rio is arranged in a wonderful construction that mixes conventional and contemporary plan components. The gallery's assortment comprises pieces by probably the most notable painters in Brazil, as well as brief displays that cover various points. Rio de Janeiro's Praça Mauá, 5 - Centro. Cost: R$20 for general entry.

The Public Exhibition Hall of Brazil is the most seasoned logical foundation in the country, having been laid out in 1818. The rich assortment of the historical centre includes antiquities and presentations that explore the regular history, ethnography, and archaic exploration of Brazil. Area: Quinta da Boa Vista in Rio de Janeiro's So Cristóvo. Cost: R$10 for general entry.

Gallery of Current Workmanship - Flamengo Park is home to the Historical centre of Present day Craftsmanship, which has a fantastic assortment of current fine art from Brazil and different nations. Ordinary discussions, film screenings, and studios are likewise held in the historical centre. Area: Parque do Flamengo, 85 Av. Infante Dom Henrique, Rio de Janeiro. Cost: R$16 for general passage.

Roberto Marinho, the maker of Globo, Brazil's most prominent media aggregate, is respected in the exhibition hall Casa Roberto Marinho, which is given to his life and heritage. The exhibition hall's assortment comprises masterpieces, furniture, and different things that Marinho assembled throughout his lifetime. Rio de Janeiro, Rua Cosme Velho, 1105 - Cosme Velho. Cost: R$10 for general entry.

The historical backdrop of Brazilian music, film, and TV is inspected at the Exhibition Hall of Picture and Sound, an interactive media establishment. Rare instruments, film reels, and different curios in the historical centre's assortment give a captivating investigation of Brazil's social history. Area: Copacabana, Rio de Janeiro, Av. Atlântica, 3432. Cost: R$12 for general entry.

Brazilian political history is investigated in presentations in the Exhibition Hall of the Republic, which is housed in the old official royal residence. From the pioneer time frame to the present, the historical centre's assortment incorporates works of art, furniture, and different antiques. Area: Rio de Janeiro, Rua do Catete, 153 - Catete. Cost: R$6 for general entry.

The set of experiences and culture of the native people groups of Brazil is the focal point of the Exhibition Hall of the Indian. The exhibition hall's assortment involves curios, pictures, and different things that portray the numerous native gatherings of Brazil's rich and fluctuating customs. Area: Botafogo, 55 Rua das Palmeiras, Rio de Janeiro. Cost: R$8 for general entry.

The Chácara do Céu Historical Center is set in a staggering manor that recently had a place with an effective Brazilian money manager. The exhibition houses various current and contemporary pieces by notable Brazilian and global craftsmen including Portinari and Di Cavalcanti. Area: St Nick Teresa, Rio de Janeiro, Rua Murtinho Nobre, 93. Cost: R$12 for general entry.

The Centro Social Banco do Brasil is a social centre point that presents an expansive scope of shows, film screenings, and live exhibitions. The middle's different programming offers all that from state-of-the-art contemporary workmanship presentations to ageless film. Area: Rio de Janeiro, Brazil, Rua Primeiro de Março, 66 - Centro. Most of the presentations are allowed to enter.

Rio de Janeiro's galleries and social establishments give something to intrigue everybody, whether they are logical fans, craftsmanship epicureans, or history buffs. Every one of these foundations, from the state-of-the-art Exhibition hall of Tomorrow to the revered Public Gallery of Brazil, gives an unmistakable and fascinating window into Brazil's set of experiences, present, and future. So make certain to incorporate several of these historical centres and social organizations on your timetable for Rio de Janeiro, and prepare to be motivated and taught by the clamouring city's rich social past.

Conclusion and Final Tips

Rio de Janeiro, in conclusion, is a city that has everything, from magnificent natural beauty to a thriving culture and history. There's never a lack of things to see and do in this intriguing city, from the recognisable beaches and mountains to the celebrated Carnival. Planning your schedule might be difficult with so many alternatives available, but with the help of our travel handbook, you have a list of the top 10 sights and activities in Rio de Janeiro.

Here are a few more suggestions to help you maximise your time in Rio de Janeiro:

Rio de Janeiro is a big metropolis with several potentially hazardous neighbourhoods, particularly at night. Make careful to check the safety of the places you want to visit and take the necessary safety measures, such as refraining from carrying valuables or going on solitary walks in remote locations.

While English is widely spoken among locals, learning a few basic Portuguese words might be useful, particularly when interacting with taxi drivers and street sellers.

You should pack some comfortable walking shoes since Rio de Janeiro is a city that is best visited on foot. Pack supportive footwear that is appropriate for walking on rough terrain.

Try the local food; it's variety and delectable. Some meals you shouldn't miss are churrasco (Brazilian-style barbeque) and feijoada (a substantial stew made with black beans and beef).

Enjoy yourself; Rio de Janeiro is a buzzing, thrilling city, and it's simple to be swept up in it. Remember to take a moment to unwind and enjoy your stay in this magnificent city.

We wish you a lovely and unforgettable stay in Rio de Janeiro and hope that our travel guide has been useful in helping you organise your vacation there!

Printed in Great Britain
by Amazon

26769194R00040